Servius and Commentary on Virgil

Pegasus
Press

PETER K. MARSHALL

Servius and Commentary on Virgil

Occasional Papers, No. 5

Pegasus Press
UNIVERSITY OF NORTH CAROLINA AT ASHEVILLE
ASHEVILLE NORTH CAROLINA
1997

Library of Congress Cataloging-in-Publication Data

Marshall, Peter K.
Servius and commentary on Virgil / Peter K. Marshall
p. cm.— (Occasional papers / Center for Medieval & Renaissance Studies ; no. 5)
Includes bibliographical references.
ISBN 1-889818-03-8 (pbk.)
I. Servius, 4th cent.—In Vergilii carmina commentarii. 2. Learning and scholarship—History—Medieval 500–1500. 3. Latin poetry—History and criticism—Theory, etc. 4. Virgil—Criticism and interpretation—History. 5. Servius, 4th cent.—Influence. 6. Rome—In literature. 7. Renaissance. I. Title. II. Series: Occasional papers (State University of New York at Binghamton, Center for Medieval & Renaissance Studies) : no. 5.
PA6823.S53M37 1997
873'.01—DC21 97-23566
CIP

For information, contact State University of New York Press, Albany, NY
www.sunypress.edu

Servius and Commentary on Virgil

Servius and Commentary on Virgil

THIS EVENING I WANT SIMPLY TO ASK a number of questions about reading Virgil. And I hasten to add that no answers will be forthcoming. It is not that I am guilty of sloth here; rather I want to make some suggestions about the ways in which further investigations might profitably be conducted, investigations which would, I suspect, take several lifetimes to complete.

When the poet Horace was bringing his first book of *Satires* to a fitting conclusion,[1] he described the ideal writer as *contentus paucis lectoribus,* and asked rhetorically "Would you, as a writer, be crazy enough to want your poetry to be read in the cheap schools? Not I," says Horace, "it's enough for me if the select few express their approval." He then names his ideal readers, one of whom, interestingly enough, is Virgil. This pose of the discriminating writer and his equally discriminating (and thus, of necessity, very small) audience

[1] Horace, *Satires* 1.10.74–76: *an tua demens/ vilibus in ludis dictari carmina malis?/ non ego: nam satis est equitem mihi plaudere.*

appears in many places in Roman antiquity, but nowhere I think more openly than here. What Virgil's thoughts were on this score is nowhere explicitly recorded. You may, if you wish, interpret the famous story of Virgil's deathbed wish[2] to destroy the *Aeneid* against such sentiment, but I myself am too hard-headed to believe that tale in the first place. What is evident is that the *Aeneid* clearly attained the status of a best-seller immediately upon its publication after Virgil's death in 19 B.C. From here it was but the slightest step to introduce the *Aeneid* as the preeminent text in the curriculum of any self-respecting Roman school. Virgil suffered the fate so feared by Horace! All too soon the intellectual world was to see the production of studies and commentaries to accompany this central expression of *Romanitas.* Of course, none of the very early ones has survived, but we do know the names of several such scholarly figures, and in some cases we have enough information at hand to know in general terms the direction in which such literary criticism went. It is immediately apparent that the great majority of such studies were laudatory, but it is worth keeping in mind that as early as the first century the scholarly Asconius Pedianus felt it appropriate to write a work *Contra obtrectatores Vergili*, and echoes of such anti-Virgilian sentiment can be found throughout antiquity. I notice, for example, that in the second century the powerful figure of Marcus Cornelius Fronto (tutor and friend to the future emperor Marcus Aurelius) seems to show a cultivated disdain for Virgil. In the whole body of his extant *Letters* (258 pages in

---

[2] This story is told most graphically in the *Life of Virgil* attributed to (Aelius) Donatus. The text may be found in J. Brummer, *Vitae Vergilianae* (Leipzig: Teubner, 1912), 9.

the most recent edition)[3] there is not a single reference to Virgil nor a single unambiguous echo.[4] It is clearly not that Fronto had not read Virgil; his marked lack of reference is assuredly quite deliberate.

But however tempting it is to speculate about Virgilian criticism in the early centuries, we are suddenly upon very solid ground by the middle of the fourth century. It is at this point that we are able to see the tantalizing figure of Aelius Donatus, who wrote a full-scale, highly detailed commentary on Virgil (amongst other Latin authors). Although this work has not survived as such, its influence is clearly felt in some of what we do have, and I am myself of the number of the faithful who believe that the so-called "longer version" of Servius is derived, seemingly directly, from this same Donatus.[5]

I want to take up the question of the two main writers on Virgil who have survived from this period, and to ask my questions about *their* work. This means inevitably that I am going to pass over the great figure of Macrobius. I call him "great" not simply because of the admirable quality of his work in that most captivating dialogue, the *Saturnalia*, but

[3] M. P. J. van den Hout, *M. Cornelius Fronto, Epistulae* (Leipzig: Teubner, 1988).

[4] The Index in van den Hout's edition lists "P. Vergilius Maro" extensively, but a close inspection will show no direct use of Virgil. Contrast the quite frequent allusions Fronto makes to the early Latin poet Ennius, who is even referred to as *Quintus noster* (van den Hout, p. 55 line 15).

[5] The evidence is lucidly presented by G. P. Goold, "Servius and the Helen Episode," *Harvard Studies in Classical Philology* 74 (1970): 101–68. Aelius Donatus, the teacher of St. Jerome, was the author of a commentary on Terence, an adaptation of which has survived: *Aeli Donati Commentum Terenti*, ed. P. Wesner, 2 vols. (Leipzig: Teubner, 1902–5).

also because of the pervasive influence he exercised throughout the Middle Ages. While this work never attained the popularity of the same author's commentary on Cicero's *Somnium Scipionis*, nevertheless there is still an impressive number of manuscripts of the *Saturnalia* extant from the Carolingian Age on,[6] and it becomes markedly popular in the twelfth century. Obviously this complex work would bear close scrutiny on many Virgilian topics, but I am excluding it here because it is not in the strict sense a "commentary," being cast in a self-consciously Platonic/Ciceronian mold as a dialogue, and ranging over a broad sweep of literary matters. It is, however, heavily Virgilian in its orientation and, as one might imagine, is strongly pro-Virgilian in its emphasis. Even those remarks to be found hostile to Virgil are clearly given to a "straw man," so that they can be effectively demolished. The tone of this work, indeed, is anything but "schoolmasterly" — the group of participants is largely aristocratic and senatorial, the values espoused are markedly those of the upper classes of Roman society, and the feeling is one of highly educated affluence.[7] In a sense, therefore, the one character I want to linger on is an anomaly — that of the celebrated *grammaticus* Servius. In Macrobius he is introduced as a modest and self-effacing, scholarly figure. Who can ever forget the wonderful way in which he is introduced, *terram intuens et*

[6] See P. K. Marshall, "Macrobius, Saturnalia," in *Texts and Transmission: A Survey of the Latin Classics*, ed. L. D. Reynolds (Oxford: Clarendon Press, 1983), 233–35.

[7] As excellently observed by Robert A. Kaster, *Guardians of Language: The Grammarian and Society in Late Antiquity* (Berkeley: Univ. of California Press, 1988), 61 ff.

velut latenti similis?[8] But he is anything but hesitant when deploying his formidable knowledge of Virgil's works, and (seemingly) any other topic even remotely relevant. Here he speaks with assured authority, and he puts aside the deference he appropriately feels in the presence of his social and political superiors.

But let us leave this scene of aristocratic ease and turn to the first of the two commentators I want to examine in greater detail. As I have indicated, my purpose is largely to raise questions and to suggest possible avenues for further investigation. The first will be Tiberius Claudius Donatus and the second will be our old friend Servius once again – perhaps a violation of chronology, but that will matter little, as neither writer shows the slightest familiarity with the work of the other, and what overlapping there is, is clearly due to their use of a common exegetical tradition. Donatus (in no way connected to Aelius Donatus, whose commentary is now lost) wrote his lengthy *Interpretationes Vergilianae*, which in the only available modern critical edition[9] runs to over 1250 pages of text and *apparatus criticus*, despite the fact that at the end he says *cursim scripsi quae potui, relinquens plurima!*,[10] in accordance with a common ancient tradition, for his son Donatianus. (We may compare the *Saturnalia* of Macrobius, among many others.) This work has been surprisingly ignored in the twentieth century. In fact there has been only one serious

[8] "Looking at the ground, like someone trying to hide."

[9] H. Georgii, *Tiberi Claudi Donati ad Tiberium Claudium Maximum Donatianum Filium Suum Interpretationes Vergilianae*, 2 vols. (Leipzig: Teubner, 1905–12; repr. Stuttgart, 1969).

[10] "I have hurriedly written what I could, omitting a great deal."

study since the above mentioned textual edition of 1905–1912.[11] It is also surprising, I believe, that it has never been translated into English, nor (as far as I am aware) into any other language. Why not? It is lengthy, to be sure, but hardly difficult to render. There would seem to be two common characterizations of the work of Donatus, neither, I would suggest, particularly helpful. First, we are told that it is virtually a paraphrase of the *Aeneid*. But surely it is much more than that: the author is greatly concerned (as his very title shows) to guide the reader into the "correct" interpretation and appreciation of Virgil's words. It is in fact instructive to see how a modern commentator (such as my own beloved teacher Roland Austin)[12] was able consistently to extract guidance from Donatus, even when he disagreed with him. It is the very act of "paraphrasing" which raises some important questions, and which compels any reader of Virgil (ancient or modern) to assent or resist.

The other frequently found description of the *Interpretationes Vergilianae* is "oratorical" or "rhetorical." Well, yes, but what is meant by either of these slippery adjectives? It is true that Donatus is much interested in the technique of oratory, as were the Romans in general and also so many writers in the Middle Ages. It is obvious that Donatus thought this a useful tool with which to analyze the *Aeneid*, and he openly

[11] Marisa Squillante Saccone, *Le Interpretationes Vergilianae di Tiberio Claudio Donato* (Naples: Società Editrice Napoletana, 1985). A concise (but not always reliable) overview is given by Giorgio Brugnoli, *Enciclopedia Virgiliana*, ed. Francesco della Corte (Rome: Istituto della Enciclopedia Virgiliana, 1985), 2:127–29.

[12] R. G. Austin produced four illuminating commentaries (on books 1, 2, 4, and 6 of the *Aeneid*) over the period 1955–77.

expresses his contempt for routine teachers and commentators in his Preface: "I have noticed that schoolteachers (*magistri*) provide no good sense to their pupils and that the writers of commentaries are motivated not by a desire to instruct, but by the wish for their own fame" (*non docendi studio, sed memoriae suae causa*).[13] It is also true that in an obvious sense the style of Donatus himself can be labeled "oratorical" — and the guess has been advanced that he was, or had been, a teacher of rhetoric. Rather than stay with this overworked term, I should myself prefer to call his style "hortatory": he is concerned to impress his reader (immediately, let us remember, his own son and anyone else of a similarly impressionable age) with a sense of *moral urgency*. The most obvious way in which this is done is to extol and glorify the figure of Aeneas, someone who is consistently motivated by the most lofty of ideals, and who emerges as a kind of *exemplum of* human perfection. Now, obviously this is a view (possibly in an extreme form) encountered ever since Virgil wrote, and certainly not unknown in the twentieth century, clearly behind the appalling remark attributed to Ezra Pound that Aeneas was "a bloody priest." But it is the consistent and enthusiastic presentation of this theme which marks the *Interpretationes* as unique.

Now, here is my first question: given this characterization, would we not expect Donatus to have been a frequently quoted writer in the Middle Ages? Just imagine the uses he could be put to in works of moral exhortation from sermons to "mirrors" of all sorts! Yet what do we in fact find? Ransacking the library collections of the world produces only three

[13] In Georgii's edition, 1:1, lines 5–7.

manuscripts from the ninth century, all French,[14] and then nothing until the fifteenth century is well under way. (I shall return to the Italian Renaissance in a moment.) Careful searches for other traces in the Middle Ages produce: a reference to the *Interpretationes* in Paul the Deacon's *Historia Langobardorum* in the late eighth century (i.e., presumably available at Montecassino?); an entry in the extant tenth-century catalogue for the library at Bobbio, also in an unattributed eleventh-century catalogue; a thirteenth-century reference to a text at Sens; and a fifteenth-century reference to what presumably was an older manuscript at Reichenau. Two years ago, Ezio Ornato pointed out that the earliest reference after these examples is still French:[15] in a letter datable to either 1400 or 1401, Jean de Montreuil (writing to Gontier Col) quotes from our Donatus. I myself have recently been able to add one tiny piece to this puzzle: while working through the nineteenth-century handwritten inventory of the manuscripts in the Vatican Library within the collection *Vaticani Latini* (I was naturally enough concerned to go carefully through those stretches where no printed catalogue has yet been produced), I stumbled across a reference to nine leaves of Donatus on *Aeneid* book 6. On calling the text up, I saw that the paper

[14] See R.H. Rouse, "Ti. Claudius Donatus," in Reynolds, 157–58.

[15] E. Ornato, "Les Humanistes français et la redécouverte des classiques," in *Préludes à la Renaissance: Aspects de la vie intellectuelle en France au XVe siècle*, ed. C. Bozzolo and E. Ornato (Paris: CNRS, 1992), esp. 13–14. Here Ornato hazards the guess that Jean de Montreuil had access to the (now lost) manuscript at Sens. The relevant portion of the text of the letter may be seen in Jean de Montreuil, *Opera*, Volume I, Parte Prima, *Epistolario*, edizione critica a cura di Ezio Ornato (Turin: Giappichelli, 1963), lines 1–3.

leaves were written in a mid-sixteenth-century hand (and I *do* wish I could date and locate it more precisely, but it does appear to be French)[16] offering what purported to be Donatus on *Aeneid* book 6, lines 1–157, a stretch which is missing in our single ninth-century Carolingian witness precisely because the first quaternion has become lost. This looked too good to be true, and I experimented for six months before I came up with what I hope is a cast-iron proof of the authenticity of this text (which would occupy about twenty pages of the standard edition).[17] So here is yet further material to which we can put the important question: *was* Donatus so little known throughout the Middle Ages? And if so, why?

You will note that other than manuscript references, the *only* literary trace is in Paul the Deacon in the late eighth century. And yet the material for sermonizing or moralizing is abundant. Let me give one telling (and, I hope, amusing) example from my recently discovered material. Line 24 of Book Six of the *Aeneid* mentions the relief on the temple depicting the monstrous story of the love of Pasiphae for the bull in Crete and the consequent birth of the Minotaur. *Hic crudelis amor tauri suppostaque furto Pasiphae* ("here the cruel love for the bull, and Pasiphae mating with him by deceit"). Donatus's comment runs: "On another part of the wall, says Virgil, Pasiphae was depicted too with the bull, which

[16] Professor Armando Petrucci, in a letter dated 30 March 1992, kindly tells me that he has examined these leaves and finds the hand to be "certainly French," dating it to 1530–50. He also observes that the watermark is similar to Briquet 8504 (Foix, 1533) and 8505 (Toulouse, 1543).

[17] For the text of these new leaves, together with the detailed proof, see P. K. Marshall, "Tiberius Claudius Donatus on Virgil Aen. 6.1–157," *Manuscripta* 37 (1993): 3–20.

(through the instigation of a cruel love) she had loved against nature (*contra institutum naturae*)." This horror expressed by Donatus is fairly routine — the story clearly lends itself to such a shocked reaction — but notice how (with a perfectly straight face) Donatus goes on to express sympathy and forgiveness for the bull! "In this act the bull mingled with the woman not of his own accord (*non sponte*), nor did he commit a sin (*nec crimen admisit*). For he suffered from a deception (*fraudem passus est*) thinking her to be an animal of his own kind." As far as I can find, this is the only place in classical antiquity where such a sentiment is expressed. It looks alarmingly theological to me — although Donatus shows not the slightest trace of any influence of Christianity anywhere else. Where *does* it come from? Collectors of erroneous, but significant, etymologies will like to know that Donatus goes on to explain why the Minotaur (the progeny resulting from this monstrous union) was so called: "Then was born the Minotaur (*Minotaurus*) so named as being less than a bull" (*minus quam taurus*),[18] the only passage in the whole of Latin literature where this splendid etymology occurs!

I am suggesting therefore that the reason why Donatus is virtually unheard of throughout the Middle Ages cannot really be that his material was in any way unpalatable. To be sure, it was not suited to use in the classroom, with its contempt for *grammatici* and its idiosyncratic methods — but it *was* rich ground from which to mine moral *exempla*. Can it be true that if one looked more carefully, citations could be found? Or is it simply that the primary manuscripts lay

[18] This fanciful derivation is clearly an error, as the vowel *i* is long in *Minotaurus*, but short in *minus*.

hidden in their monastic libraries for centuries? Clearly there would be parallels for such undeserved and accidental obscurity, and such a fate would hardly appear to be surprising. This is, in fact, what I had been content to believe, until I came to ask the same question from the other end.

Let us now jump on to the fifteenth century and witness the "rebirth" of the *Interpretationes Vergilianae.* As in so many cases, Italy was the scene of the rediscovery of this text, but by a slightly odd route: one manuscript of books 1–5, now in the Laurentian Library in Florence,[19] was transported to Italy from France in 1438 by Jean Jouffroy (why? one wonders in vain); the second manuscript, now in the Vatican Library (containing books 6–12),[20] came likewise from France, somewhere around 1460, in whose hands we do not know. Yet if we expected vast excitement and enthusiasm to surround this recovery, we are going to be strongly disappointed by the surviving evidence. I have combed all the possible libraries to uncover fifteenth-century manuscripts, and have come up with *only twelve*, of which only five contain (or ever contained) all twelve books, the rest being of one half or the other. Why on earth is this? Clearly the opportunity was there for copies to be made. Either we have to assume that numerous copies were made and have subsequently disappeared, or else we have to explain the small numbers some

[19] Florence, Biblioteca Medicea Laurenziana 45.15. For a fuller account of Donatus in the fifteenth century, see P.K. Marshall, "Tiberius Claudius Donatus in the Fifteenth Century," in *Tria Lustra: Essays and Notes Presented to John Pinsent*, Liverpool Classical Papers, no. 3 (Liverpool, 1993), 325–28. To the list of manuscripts given there now may be added Vatican Library, Vat. lat. 7582.

[20] Vatican Library, Vat. lat. 1512.

other way. The separate, complete printed edition was not to come until 1535, but Donatus, at least in some part, did feature in editions of Virgil from the end of the fifteenth century.[21] As my fellow investigator, Craig Kallendorf, observes with some pain, "After all, Vegio's *Book XIII* survives in some 48 manuscripts, so the 12 for Donatus is really quite striking."[22] So we appear to be left with a puzzle at the beginning and at the end of the Middle Ages. Clearly more work remains to be done, but I feel certain that it should be done by serious medievalists, not by classical dabblers like me!

If we may take Tiberius Claudius Donatus to be a good example of an author who ought to have been popular throughout the Middle Ages, but who never was, then we may surely come back to Servius as a splendid example of a writer who was (and beyond any doubt, deservedly) popular and widely used throughout the Middle Ages, into the Renaissance and finally into the age of the printed book. His influence was enormous. From my own work I can attest, for example, to the profound debt owed to him by Isidore of Seville, not merely in the *Etymologiae*,[23] but also in the *De differentiis*;[24] so much

[21] G. Mambelli, *Gli Annali delle Edizioni Virgiliane* (Florence: Olschki, 1954), lists an edition of Virgil from 1484 (no. 51) as the first to contain notes from Donatus. The first complete Donatus was printed in 1535 at Naples (Mambelli no. 174).

[22] In a letter dated 14 April 1994.

[23] This debt is not readily apparent if one uses the only complete modern edition of the *Etymologiae*, the Oxford Classical Text of W. M. Lindsay, 2 vols., 1911. The re-edition, with translation and commentary, of all twenty books of the *Etymologiae*, in twenty separate volumes, now in progress, will give a much more complete picture.

[24] Isidoro de Sevilla, *Diferencias, Libro I*, Introducción, Edición Critica, Traducción y Notas, Carmen Codoñer (Paris: Les Belles Lettres, 1992).

so that in many places an editor of Servius has to accord Isidore the authority of an early seventh-century manuscript.[25] Similarly, amongst the many sources of that invaluable collection of annotations to Statius's *Thebaid* attributed to one Lactantius Placidus, there once again is felt the powerful presence of Servius. Alas, we know all too little of the date, location, or indeed authorship of this "commentary" of Lactantius Placidus, but I must say that I eagerly await the appearance of the new critical edition by Dale Sweeney, which is announced by Teubner — almost a century after the only modern edition accessible, that by Jahnke from 1898.[26] I feel sure that much is likely to be discovered from a careful comparison of a reasonable text of Lactantius Placidus and his several sources — if that indeed proves to be the direction of the derivation! Then again, that strange and sprawling amalgam of mythographical material know as the "Vatican Mythographers" owes a great debt to Servius, and once again (at least in the case of the first — and earliest — mythographer) this work can very well be accorded the status of an early manuscript witness for Servius. As with Lactantius Placidus, we are fortunate to have a very recent new critical edition, that of Peter Kulcsár, at least for the first two Mythographers.[27]

---

[25] As Isidore died in the year 636, with his work not yet officially "published," this gives a clear terminus ante quem for the date of the manuscript(s) of Servius he drew upon.

[26] *Lactantii Placidi qui dicitur commentarios in Statii Thebaida et commentarium in Achilleida* recensuit R. Jahnke (Leipzig: Teubner, 1898).

[27] Previously there was available only the edition of G. H. Bode, *Scriptores rerum mythicarum latini tres Romae nuper reperti*, Celle, 1834; now see P. Kulcsár, *Mythographi Vaticani I et II*, Corpus Christianorum, Series Latina XCIc (Turnhout: Brepols, 1987).

As you may know, I work with the manuscripts of Servius, and I can, from what I hope is exhaustive personal experience, attest to the vast numbers of texts surviving from the beginnings to well into the fifteenth century. I have seen literally hundreds of them, and they survive from many periods and many different geographical regions. The most ancient, in fact, is an early-eighth-century fragment, a series of excerpts in an English hand, a fragment from a binding now to be found in the Staatsarchiv in Marburg.[28] As might be expected, the *form* in which Servius is presented assumed many different aspects, and this is an area which I wish someone would investigate in detail, because this very variety (so annoying in fact to someone like me, someone who is searching for the *ipsissima verba* of Servius!) nevertheless tells us that Servius was, in many ways, a *living* text — by which I mean that he was clearly *used*, clearly adapted and "improved upon" (if I may dare say so) over the centuries.[29] This is something which rarely happens in the transmission of a text from classical antiquity; maybe a vague parallel can be drawn with some dramatic works, such as the *Comedies* of Plautus, but the reasons there are quite different.

Let me just look at some shapes in which Servius has survived, and see what they might possibly tell us about his medieval reception. As far as I am aware, it has never been proved exactly how the original was presented. Most people

[28] Previously listed as "Spangenberg, Pfarrenbibliothek," this precious witness is now accessible in the Hessisches Staatsarchiv, Marburg.

[29] Since this talk was given, there has appeared the splendid study of Christopher Baswell, *Virgil in Medieval England: Figuring the Aeneid from the Twelfth Century to Chaucer* (Cambridge: Cambridge Univ. Press, 1995), which takes up many aspects of this and other related questions.

simply assume that the work was published *separately* from the text of Virgil on which it comments, line by line, and often word by word. If this is indeed the case, then it may have some important consequences. I think, for example, of a fairly recent French study of the presence of manuscripts of the works of Virgil in certain medieval libraries.[30] At one point we are told that, although the presence of Virgil is not specifically attested, the library *must* have had him *because we know that they had a text of Servius*! The innocent assumption behind this form of reasoning I find highly intriguing. Is it in fact the case that people read Servius solely as a commentary on Virgil? People most certainly do *not* follow this pattern today, and I should be astonished if they ever felt themselves so confined once classical antiquity came to an end. There is such a rich variety of subject-matter to be found in Servius that it would hardly be surprising to see the *Commentaries* leading a life somewhat independent of Virgil. I notice, for example, that in the surviving *Letters* of the ninth-century abbot of Ferrières, Servatus Lupus, a man of no inconsiderable erudition and a passionate lover of antiquity, Servius is as often quoted (sometimes even anonymously) of himself, as he is for his explication of Virgil.[31] It is precisely this independent existence which will lead, in the fifteenth century for example, to works such as the *Vocabularium* (attributed to Guarino) drawn from Servius, of which several copies survive.[32]

---

[30] *Lectures médiévales de Virgile* (Collection de l'école française de Rome, 80), Rome, 1985. The remark occurs on p. 14 of the article by Louis Holtz: "La redécouverte de Virgile aux VIIIe et IXe siècles," 9–30.

[31] See the passages listed in *Servati Lupi Epistulae*, ed. P. K. Marshall (Leipzig: Teubner, 1984), 139.

[32] To be found, for example, in the Vatican, Reg. lat. 1836, fols. 93–153.

I should like also to note that I have come across several fifteenth-century Italian manuscripts of pure Servius (i.e., with no text of Virgil), which contain a kind of marginal commentary on Servius[33] — commentary on a commentary! My initial suspicion, from the hands involved, is that this is Florentine in origin. I greatly hope that it will prove possible to discover who the author was.

But secondly we should also be aware that Servius has survived from the early ninth century onwards *also* in a form grafted onto the text of Virgil — a considerable feat if we consider the planning and arrangement implicit in getting the two texts to line up in a way satisfactory for the reader.

Under a third heading I would put anything which might reasonably be described as "excerpts" from Servius. Clearly there is great variety here — from a sort of "abbreviated" Servius to very meager citations, often just a note or two. I suspect much could be elicited from a bringing together of such material: it would seem to me likely that such a study would reveal a great deal about the readership of Virgil at certain periods, and also about the teaching of Virgil in the classroom.

In a fourth division I bring together what are sometimes termed "notes drawn from Servius" or "showing Servian influence," and surely these are of great interest, as they show the Mediaeval reader/commentator *refashioning* Servius to suit a particular need. Indeed it is obvious that virtually any commentary could be so described, even some in this century. Under this heading I would place the work of so-called Philar-

[33] An example of this form of commentary may be seen in Paris, Bibliothèque Ste. Geneviève, MS. 1116.

gyrius on the *Eclogues* (clearly a Christian work)[34] or such collections as the *Berne Scholia.*[35] But notice that it is not at all unusual to have two or more strands of commentary either freestanding or surrounding one text of Virgil. An early example of this phenomenon would be the Laon manuscript 468 from the ninth century (available in facsimile with some fascinating analysis by J. Contreni),[36] which contains *inter alia* excerpts from Virgil combined with glosses from other sources, including Philargyrius, or else "adaptations" with an eventual Servian origin. Clearly a collection of comments and notes designed for school use, as Contreni shows. A further celebrated example would be Petrarch's Virgil in the Ambrosian Library in Milan, in which we find Servius together with Virgil, but also other notes, some of them Petrarch's own.[37] As Mary L. Lord has recently demonstrated,[38] a late fourteenth-century manuscript in the Biblioteca Casanatense in Rome is closely associated with this Ambrosian book, containing some Servius, some Petrarch and in addition some commentary by Benvenuto da Imola. Layer upon layer!

---

[34] This is to be found in vol. 3 of *Servii grammatici qui feruntur in Vergilii carmina commentarii,* ed. G. Thilo et H. Hagen (Leipzig: Teubner, 1887).

[35] *Scholia Bernensia ad Vergili Bucolica atque Georgica,* ed. H. Hagen, (Leipzig: Teubner, 1867; repr. Georg Olms, Hildesheim, 1967).

[36] *Codex Laudunensis 468: A Ninth-Century Guide to Virgil, Sedulius, and the Liberal Arts,* John J. Contreni, Armarium Codicum Insignium, vol. 3 (Turnhout: Brepols, 1984).

[37] Available in the facsimile published by G. Galbiati, *Francisci Petrarchae Vergilianus codex quam simillime expressus* (Milan, 1930).

[38] "The Commentary on Virgil's *Eclogues* by Benvenuto da Imola: a comparative study of the *Recollectiones,*" *Euphrosyne* 22 (1994): 373–401, particularly 378–79 for the manuscript Biblioteca Casanatense 960.

So very much remains to be done on Servius and the way he meant his work to be read, and how in fact it *was* read. It may seem surprising that the last attempt at a comprehensive study of Servius was done in 1880 by Emile Thomas, *Essai sur Servius* — a wonderfully suggestive work,[39] but inevitably trying to do too much in too confined a space. Since the early decades of this century, a great deal of attention has been paid to purely textual matters — clearly an important interest, which has so far resulted in many revealing studies of the manuscripts, and so far two volumes of the projected five of the "Harvard Servius" (one in 1946, the other in 1965).[40] To be sure, a handful of studies (largely rather mechanical and pedestrian dissertations)[41] have appeared on individual topics, but nothing in any way designed to give us a broad and persuasive understanding of this influential work.

Any such investigation would not lack for subjects to treat. One could, for example, imagine an enormously fascinating section on religion, a subject which receives great emphasis in the pages of Servius. Why? What effect was this designed to produce on the schoolchild of the late fourth century?[42]

---

[39] *Essai sur Servius et son commentaire sur Virgile* (Paris, 1880).

[40] *Servianorum in Vergilii carmina commentariorum editionis Harvardianae volumen II* (on *Aeneid* 1 and 2), E.K. Rand et al. (Lancaster, 1946); *volumen III* (on *Aeneid* 3–5), A.F. Stocker and A.H. Travis (Oxford, 1965).

[41] See, for example, the items listed by Giorgio Brugnoli in the *Enciclopedia Virgiliana*, 4:812–13.

[42] Note the astute observation made by Charles E. Murgia that Tiberius Claudius Donatus speaks of Roman (pagan) religious practices as still current in his day, whereas Servius speaks of them in the past tense: "*Aen.* 9.236 — An Unrecognized Vergilian Variation," *Hermes* 116 (1988): 493–99, especially 496 n. 5. What, one wonders, does this tell us about the relative dates of these two writers?

What picture of the Roman world did it create for the medieval reader? Or again, what about the notes on philosophy? Why does the modern reader get the impression that in such sections Servius is so jejune as to suggest a strong lack of interest on his part (despite his perfectly correct assertion that Virgil was steeped in philosophical reading; just look at his remarks prefatory to his commentary on book 6 of the *Aeneid*)? Did Servius have any effect on the medieval understanding of Stoicism or Epicureanism, for example, two schools whose views he so frequently cites? Again, what about law? Why is there so little attention given to this eminently Roman subject? Or what about Servius's criteria deployed in his literary criticism? Here we do have an admirable (and, as far as I can see, virtually unknown) Yale dissertation by Philip Lockhart (1959), who, I am sure, would be the first to admit that numerous questions lie untouched.[43]

But let me concentrate just a little more closely on three topics which could certainly stand much more probing than they have so far received. Again, I offer these suggestions not simply in the hope of understanding Servius in his own right, but also of trying to get some sense of how influential he could be or should have been for readers throughout the succeeding centuries.

The most obvious of all is "language" in the widest possible sense, ranging from etymology (on which we now have the aid of that invaluable book *A Lexicon of Ancient Latin Etymologies* by Robert Maltby)[44] to grammar, to syntax, to

[43] Philip N. Lockhart, "The literary criticism of Servius," Ph.D. diss., Yale University, 1959.

[44] Leeds: Francis Cairns Publications, 1991.

the interrelationship of Greek and Latin literature. As may have been indicated by my earlier remarks, this is precisely the area where we see Servius living a life of his own (at least potentially), when the value of his writing becomes independent of its connection with Virgil, as I suggested, by way of example, in the case of Servatus Lupus. Even though we can see Servius occasionally getting it wrong,[45] he is none the less impressive in his lofty magisterial pose. Just consider how many notes begin with the intimidating "You should be aware," *sciendum est*! In his recent book *Guardians of Language* Robert Kaster has many astute remarks on Servius;[46] he constantly asks just the right questions and offers some excellent answers. I am particularly struck, in this regard, by his insistence on our noticing that so very often Servius gives more (much more?) information than is needed simply for the elucidation of the text of Virgil. Why is this? Kaster suggests that, from his position of high authority, Servius is concerned to *teach*, to teach language, history, or whatever it is, not simply Virgil. But there is a refinement which I think can be added to this acute observation, and it is one pointed out thirty-five years ago by the wrongly neglected Lockhart, who raised the simple question: "For what audience did Servius write?" Time and time again, the obvious answer has been given "For schoolboys," but Lockhart seems to me convincing in his rejection of this view and the substitution of the answer "For school*teachers*," that is to say *magistri*, *gramma-*

[45] For example, he clearly does not understand that in Virgil's day the final *-o* in the ablative case of gerunds was by nature long. See his fumbling comment at *Aen.* 4.413.

[46] See above, n. 7.

tici. If this understanding is correct, then it will render all the more explicable the process by which Servius was transformed — rewritten, abridged, whatever — in later centuries.

A second area where I suspect much remains to be done is "history."[47] Now, much can be said about Servius's perfectly correct insistence that, in effect, schoolchildren should know their history, and particularly in connection with the *Eclogues* or the *Georgics* or the *Aeneid*. We can forgive him for the occasional slip. For example, he is the only ancient writer I know who gets the date of Julius Caesar's assassination wrong.[48] We all know it was the Ides of March, and one wonders where on earth Servius found the date May 13th! But there are two areas of "history" where I should like to see some further investigation. One revolves around the question: how far did Servius understand the reign of the man we refer to as the emperor Augustus? Or, to put the question more pointedly, to what extent did he read back from his own age in the late fourth century and see in Augustus the form of a much later ruler? Let me just look at one note to illustrate my concern. In the famous "Parade of Heroes" in book 6 of the *Aeneid*, at line 841 Anchises addresses *te, magne Cato*. Servius hastens to assure us that the Cato referred to here must be the old fellow Cato Censorius.[49] I should certainly agree with

---

[47] See now the excellent article by David B. Dietz, "*Historia* in the Commentary of Servius," *Transactions of the American Philological Association* 125 (1995): 61–97.

[48] His comment in the introduction to the *Eclogues* (p. 2, line 25, ed. Thilo) reads: *post occisum III iduum Maiarum die in senatu Caesarem*. Attempts to explain away this error as a textual corruption have proved singularly unconvincing.

[49] He lived 234–149 B.C.

him, but *not* for the reason he gives: "For he [Virgil] could not have praised Cato Uticensis[50] in the presence of Augustus, as the Emperor's father [Julius Caesar] both fought against him and wrote the *Anticatones*." This I find to be a very rigid and unresponsive view of the relationship between Virgil and Augustus, especially as in this selfsame passage Virgil has felt free to mention both Julius Caesar *and* his great foe Pompey, with the further plea that Julius Caesar should be the first to throw down his arms.[51] So I should like to see some exploration of Servius's understanding of the reign of the emperor as opposed to the Respublica.

The other area where much could be said is one in which I think Servius did serious damage to subsequent readers of Virgil. This is his all too frequent insistence that Virgilian characters "stand for" people in the real, external Roman world. Most damage, I suggest, has been to the reading of the *Eclogues*, and I further believe that so much of the nonsense we read in the ancient "Lives of Virgil" is due to this form of reading — not one, to be sure, originating with Servius, but one which is remarkably alive in medieval commentators such as Philargyrius, wherein such "allegorization" (if that is indeed the proper term) takes on a powerful form.

The third (and final) area in which I would suggest the need and opportunity for much further investigation, is that of "Mythology." It was clearly a theme dear to Servius's heart. As would have been only appropriate (and presumably also necessary) for his imagined schoolchild/schoolmaster, he

---

[50] The Cato who gained immortality by committing suicide after Julius Caesar's crushing victory at Utica in 46 B.C.

[51] *Aen.* 6.826–35.

gives us a vast array of mythological information. A good example would be the note to *Aeneid* 6.14: *Daedalus ut fama est fugiens Minoia regna*, where the mass of information produces one of his longest notes, going all the way back to the adulterous affair of Mars and Venus, and ending with one of his not infrequent assertions that most myths originated in "real" situations with "real" people. I have already indicated just a few of the later authors indebted to Servius, and I mentioned Isidore of Seville, the Vatican Mythographers and the so-called Lactantius Placidus on the *Thebaid* of Statius. There are, of course, very many more, and the progression of such indebtedness would repay careful investigation. However, I should like to make one general observation of caution about the way in which I have noticed some scholars write about any medieval indebtedness to classical writers on mythology. This is: before any assertion of such indebtedness can be made, it should first be established that the text(s) in question were available. Let me give a few examples, beginning with an author who has exercised me much over the last several years, that is Hyginus, the author of the *Fabulae*.[52] Now, if all my work revealed one thing,[53] it was that clearly this text was in extremely short supply throughout the Middle Ages (and

[52] He may, or may not, be identical with the Hyginus who wrote the *Astronomica*, a work which by contrast *did* have a wide medieval circulation. See M. D. Reeve in Reynolds 187–89. Since Reeve's article, no fewer than two critical editions of the *Astronomica* have appeared: *Hygin, l'Astronomie: texte établi et traduit par André Le Boeuffle*, Société d'Edition "Les Belles Lettres" (Paris, 1983); *Hyginus, De Astronomia*, ed. Gh. Viré (Stuttgart and Leipzig: Teubner, 1992).

[53] See *Hyginus, Fabulae*, ed. P. K. Marshall (Stuttgart: Teubner, 1993), with the facts summarized in the *Praefatio* and presented fully throughout the text among the *Testimonia*.

indeed was not to appear as a printed text until 1535). But what do we find? In 1963 Guido Guarino published his English translation of Boccaccio's *Concerning Famous Women* (the *De mulieribus claris*) with introduction and notes.[54] At the end of this volume come five pages listing Boccaccio's "sources" for this work. For the first thirty-eight stories, or chapters, Guarino lists no fewer than forty-one chapters of Hyginus among these "sources." But the simplest of examinations of all these supposed derivations shows nothing of the sort. The same mythological stories are indeed to be found, but there is not the *slightest* indication that Boccaccio had ever set eyes upon the work of Hyginus. Ovid surely, but not the author of the *Fabulae*.

Again, as careful a scholar as M. C. Seymour in his splendid, many-volume edition of the English text of John Trevisa's translation of Bartholomaeus Anglicus *On the properties of things* (*De proprietatibus rerum*),[55] in one passage makes the mistake of supposing that Bartholomaeus is quoting from this work of Hyginus in the thirteenth century. This is clearly *not* the case.

Much more recently there has been published a vast and ambitious work entitled *Medieval Mythography*,[56] which is

---

[54] *Concerning Famous Women. By Giovanni Boccaccio*, trans. with an introduction and notes by Guido A. Guarino (New Brunswick: Rutgers Univ. Press, 1963).

[55] The error can be found in the volume entitled *Bartholomaeus Anglicus and his Encyclopedia*, M. C. Seymour and Colleagues (Variorum, 1992), 113, where a close examination of the text shows that Seymour has (understandably enough) been misled into thinking that Bartholomaeus had read the *Fabulae*. Surely the reference is to the readily available *Astronomica*.

[56] Jane Chance, *Medieval Mythography: From Roman North Africa to*

full of fascinating material and which will surely repay close attention. Yet the warning signs are there to be seen. Thus we are told (165) that the First Vatican Mythographer contains "a handful of glosses from Hyginus's *Fabulae*." No evidence is given, nor, I believe, does any exist for this assertion. The plain fact is that so much of these Mythographers is drawn from Servius. Even more astounding, to me at least, is another note (171) that "the Berne scholia [i.e., to Virgil's *Eclogues* and *Georgics*] may have influenced ... Christine de Pizan's *Epistre Othea*" — again, no evidence offered.

But to come back for one final moment to Servius. Nowhere, I think, is it clearer that he simply enjoys providing more than enough information to his readers, than it is in those notes where he shows his vast interest in mythology. The huge number of Virgilian manuscripts I have seen carrying glosses from Servius on mythological subjects is witness enough to his long and undiminished life throughout the Middle Ages.

I greatly hope that at least some of the themes I have looked at in general terms will be made more challenging and yet more accessible by the eventual publication of two works of collaborative effort. The first is the final three volumes of the "Harvard Servius." While it would be overly optimistic to say that publication is "imminent," much work has been completed, and we may indeed see these volumes in the near future. The second is the volume of the series *Catalogus Translationum et Commentariorum* to be devoted to Virgil, in which every commentary (as well as translation) from the

the School of Chartres, A.D. 433–1177 (Gainesville: Univ. of Florida Press, 1994).

beginning up to the year 1600 will be listed, with *all* known manuscripts. I trust that, armed with these new tools, investigators braver than I will push on with the study of Servius himself and of his huge influence.

Appendix A

Servius the Man

DESPITE THE WIDESPREAD POPULARITY OF HIS WORK, very little is known about the life of Servius.[57] Indeed, there is some uncertainty about his full name. In the earliest manuscripts of the *Commentaries*, he is referred to simply as "Servius." Thus a text in the University Library in Leiden[58] has as the subscription to the *Commentary* on book 5 of the *Aeneid*: EXPLICIT LIBER QUINTUS EXPOSITIONUM SERVII GRAMMATICI IN LIBRUM QUINTUM AENEIDUM. Later texts will occasionally add "Maurus" (or "Marius") and "Honoratus," but these are clearly derived from other works attributed to a Servius and have no unambiguous authority for the author of the *Commentaries*.

---

[57] The full evidence is presented and carefully weighed by Kaster, 356–59. See also Giorgio Brugnoli in the *Enciclopedia Virgiliana*, 4:805–13.

[58] B.P.L. 52. See the facsimile in G. I. Lieftinck, *Servii grammatici in Vergilii carmina commentarii: Codex Leidensis B.P.L.52* (Amsterdam: North-Holland Publishing Company, 1960 [= Umbrae Codicum Occidentalium I], fol. 15r. Note that in the *Saturnalia* Macrobius also uses only the name "Servius."

It is only reasonable to accept that he is the Servius who figures so prominently in the *Saturnalia* of Macrobius. There he is presented as a "young" man (7.11.2), an *adulescens* as opposed to a *senex*, but these are vague terms at best. In addition, the dramatic date of the *Saturnalia* (in the 380s) is not much help, as Macrobius explicitly says (1.1.5) that he is taking liberties with chronological verisimilitude after the model of Plato in his dialogues.

However, while it is impossible to put precise dates to the life of Servius, it is of great importance to set him against the two other writers on Virgil of roughly the same period. It is very clear that Servius is writing his *Commentaries* after the work of Aelius Donatus,[59] as he refers to his predecessor's work (often in marked disagreement) on numerous occasions. The period of high activity for Aelius Donatus was in the 350s and 360s.

Servius's relationship to the other writer, Tiberius Claudius Donatus,[60] is of much less importance, as neither author makes even the slightest allusion to the other in the course of their extensive works.[61]

---

[59] On whom see Kaster, 275–78. Some indication of the frequency of his name in Servius can be gained from J. F. Mountford and J. T. Schultz, *Index rerum et nominum in scholiis Servii et Aelii Donati tractatorum*, Cornell Studies in Classical Philology, vol. 23 (Ithaca: Cornell Univ. Press, 1930). The entry "Donatus" on p. 56 has forty-seven references to the text of Servius.

[60] See Kaster, 400. It has already been suggested (n. 41 above) that this Donatus also was writing before Servius.

[61] With this in mind, it is interesting to note that these two writers first appear together in the ninth century, in the extensive marginal and interlinear notes in the so-called "Virgil of Tours," Berne, Burgerbibliothek 165.

Appendix B

Reading Servius

TO SHOW SERVIUS AT WORK more clearly, to point out the wide range of his interests, to demonstrate his strengths and his failings, it will be helpful to look at a representative portion of his *Commentaries,* namely that on the first ten lines of the fourth book of the *Aeneid.* A translation is given for each note, although the virtual impossibility of presenting a consistent version of such a work is all too evident. Where the subject matter involves minute grammatical detail, for example, it has seemed preferable to leave some words or phrases in the original Latin. Some observations follow each note. These are not in any sense intended to provide a commentary on the *Commentaries.* They rather attempt to point up the ways in which Servius goes about his task.

The Latin text used is that of volume 3 of the Harvard Servius (*Servianorum in Vergilii carmina commentariorum editionis Harvardianae volumen III),* edited by A.F. Stocker and A.H. Travis (Oxford, 1965). As this discussion is of Servius proper, no attention has been paid to the "fuller" version, sometimes referred to as "Servius Danielis" or "DServ," which is also to be found in the Harvard Servius.

1. Apollonius Argonautica scripsit et in tertio inducit amantem Medeam; inde totus hic liber translatus est. est autem paene totus in affectione, licet in fine pathos habeat, ubi abscessus Aeneae gignit dolorem. sane totus in consiliis et subtilitatibus est; nam paene comicus stilus est; nec mirum, ubi de amore tractatur. iunctus quoque superioribus est, quod artis esse videtur, ut frequenter diximus; nam ex abrupto vitiosus est transitus. licet stulte quidam dicunt hunc tertio non esse coniunctum — in illo enim navigium, in hoc amores exsequitur — non videntes optimam coniunctionem; cum enim tertium sic clauserit *factoque hic fine quievit*, intulit *at regina gravi iamdudum saucia cura*, item paulo post (5) *nec placidam membris dat cura quietem*; nam cum Aenean dormire dixerit, satis congrue subiunxit ut somno amans careret.

1. Apollonius wrote the *Argonautica*, and in the third book he introduces Medea in love. From this was taken the whole of this book [i.e., *Aeneid* 4]. It is almost wholly concerned with emotion, although at the end it involves pathos, when the departure of Aeneas creates anguish. It centers wholly on planning and subtlety; for the style is almost that of comedy. Nor is this surprising where the theme is love. It is also connected to the previous books [i.e., *Aeneid* 1–3]. This is evidently in accordance with the precepts of art, as we have often remarked. For an abrupt transition is faulty, although some people foolishly claim that it is not connected to book 3 (for in that book Virgil describes a sea-voyage,

> in this book a love affair). These people do not see the excellent connection. For after ending book 3 with "here he ended and rested," he then starts "But the Queen, long wounded with heavy care," and shortly afterwards "nor does her care give calm rest to her limbs." For after saying that Aeneas slept, quite appropriately he added how a lover could not sleep.

Servius begins his remarks with a prefatory paragraph on book 4 as a whole. This is not his normal practice: for the *Aeneid* we find such prefaces only to book 1 (although that is actually an introduction to the entire *Commentary* on the *Aeneid*), 3, 4, 6, and 7. Of these, the matter on 3 and 7 is comparatively slight.

Here Servius starts with a general observation on the relationship between Virgil's creation and the *Argonautica* of Apo-llonius of Rhodes. It is a typically authoritarian comment, broad in outline and employing little or no qualification. He chooses to ignore other obvious influences on Virgil, such as the *Medea* of Euripides, and presents an exaggerated view of the importance of Apollonius. The parallels are indeed numerous: the plot of Aphrodite/Venus, getting Eros/Cupid to shoot his arrow into the female victim Medea/Dido (a scene actually found at the end of *Aeneid* book 1, before the action of book 4); the obliging, complacent sister (Chalciope in Apollonius, Anna in Virgil); the threatening figure of the brother (Apsyrtus in Apollonius, killed by Jason; Pygmalion in Virgil, still very much alive); the scene in the cave. Many other parallels and even minute verbal echoes can be found, but Servius does not direct the reader's attention to the huge differences between the works. Thus it should be pointed out that the account of Apollonius stops long before there is any question of Medea's being abandoned by Jason, whereas in Virgil the happiness of the two lovers is very short-lived. But above all the modern reader misses some discussion of the ways in which Virgil took inspiration from a work which is, let it be confessed, remarkably second-rate, and turned so many of Apollonius's suggestions into a powerful and compelling work of his own. It may seem surprising that Servius does not take up the question of this literary influence at any other point in this book, but this is all too typical a part of his magisterial manner.

The reference to comedy may strike a modern reader as odd: is not this book in so many ways remarkably tragic? But it should be remembered that the extant comedies of Plautus and Terence already show many of the features which were later to become standard fare in the Latin love elegy (Tibullus, Propertius, and Ovid, as well as works which have not survived).

Servius's own concern with the transition from one book to another again shows his magisterial pose, dismissing those who refuse to see Virgil's deftness as "foolish." This high-handed approach comes out in the all too characteristic "as we have often remarked," a turn of phrase which, in one form or another, occurs throughout the Commentary.

We may also wonder at the bizarre interpretation Servius gives to the final word of book 3 of the *Aeneid*, where he takes *quievit* to mean "went off to sleep," rather than the obvious "rested," i.e., "stopped speaking." Although there has been the occasional modern commentator who accepts Servius's understanding, most would agree that it comes pretty close to a blunder — something by no means unparalleled in these sprawling *Commentaries*.

IAMDVDVM aut 'nimium', ut Terentius *iamdudum te amat; iamdudum illi facile sit quod doleat*; aut *iamdudum*, a quo tempore vidit Aenean – legimus enim (I 613) *obstipuit primo aspectu Sidonia Dido.*

IAMDVDVM Either "exceedingly," as Terence [*Eunuchus* 448] *iamdudum te amat; iamdudum illi facile sit quod doleat;* or *iamdudum* means "ever since she first saw Aeneas." For we read (*Aen.* 1.613] "Sidonian Dido was astonished at first sight."

This note exhibits one of Servius's more charming tendencies: the willingness to present a variety of possible interpretations of a single word, as here, or a phrase. Again the reader is presented with a puzzle: the word *iamdudum* can hardly be glossed as *nimium* ("exceedingly"), and it certainly does not mean this in the parallel quoted from Terence. The second explanation, "for a long time now," is clearly the correct one.

SAVCIA hinc subiungit *vulnus alit*. et bene adludit ad Cupidinis tela, ut paulo post ad faculam, *et caeco carpitur igni*; nam sagittarum vulnus est, facis incendium.

SAVCIA Hence he adds "she feeds the wound." And he cleverly alludes to Cupid's weapon, as he does shortly afterwards to the torch, "and she is consumed with the hidden fire." For the wound comes from the arrows, the fire from the torch.

A typically brief, but none the less highly important observation. It invites the reader to be alert to the imagery of wounding and of fire, which so powerfully distinguishes this book, culminating in the great scene where Dido stabs herself on the pyre she has built.

CVRA amore; ab eo quod cor urat, ut (X 132) *Veneris iustissima cura*, item (I 678) *mea maxima cura*.

CVRA "Love," derived from *cor urat* ("it burns the heart"), as [*Aen.* 10.132] *Veneris iustissima cura*, also [*Aen.* 1.678] *mea maxima cura*.

Although this etymology is simply fanciful, the significance of such beliefs for the Roman mind should not be underestimated. In fact, this etymology could very well have been known to Virgil himself, as its first appearance comes in his slightly older contemporary, the great scholar Marcus Terentius Varro, *De Lingua Latina* 6.46: *cura, quod cor urat*. The importance of etymology for Servius, as a means of revealing hidden meaning, is vast and persistent. Some indication of its scope in Servius and other Roman writers may be seen in great detail in Robert Maltby, *A Lexicon of Ancient Latin Etymologies* (Leeds: Francis Cairns Publications, 1991).

2. VENIS quia per venas amor currit sicut venemum; inde dictum (I 688) *fallasque veneno*, item (I 749) *longumque bibebat amorem*.

2. VENIS Because love runs through the veins [*venas*] like poison [*venenum*]. Hence it is written [*Aen.* 1.688] "you deceive with poison," likewise [*Aen.* 1.747] "she drank a deep draught of love."

While this is not quite an etymology, the explanation does involve a play on the words *vena* and *venenum*, for which see Maltby (quoted in the last note) p. 634, s.v. *"venenum."*

CAECO CARPITVR IGNI agit Vergilius ut inventas frangat declamationes, ut hoc loco rem dixit sine declamatione; unde Ovidius *quoque magis tegitur, tanto magis aestuat ignis. caeco* ergo *igni* 'validiore', cuius natura est ut compressus magis convalescat.

CAECO CARPITVR IGNI Virgil is concerned to avoid artistic declamation; so in this passage he has described the matter without any declamation. Hence Ovid [*Metamorphoses* 4.64] "The more it is hidden, the more the fire blazes." So by "hidden fire" he means "more powerful," as it is the nature of fire to gain strength if it is suppressed.

A somewhat mysterious note, which seems to mean that here Virgil varies from his practice of portraying emotions through the use of speeches. As the *Commentaries* pay deserved attention to the power of oratory through all the works of Virgil, it is important to observe that here Servius acknowledges the purely descriptive energy discernible in this passage.

MVLTA VIRI VIRTUS ANIMO bene mediam se facit praebere Didonem inter regalem pudorem et amoris inpulsum. simulat enim se virtutem mirari, cuius pulchritudine commovetur. *multa* autem *virtus* figurate dixit; nam ad numerum transtulit quod est quantitatis.

MVLTA VIRI VIRTUS ANIMO He excellently makes Dido reveal herself as caught between royal modesty and the goading of love. For she pretends that she admires his valor, when she is moved by his looks. He has used the phrase *multa virtus* figuratively; for he has transferred a quantitative idea to a numerical one.

The enthusiasm of Servius for his author is one of his most endearing characteristics. His usual method of expressing such approbation is by the use of a laudatory adverb, particularly (as here) *bene.*

The remark that *multa* ["much"] is used as an equivalent to *magna* ["great"] may strike a modern reader as pedantic, but it is precisely this kind of glossing which can be found in so many Virgilian manuscripts throughout the Middle Ages.

> RECVRSAT bene frequentativo usus est verbo in frequenti amantis cogitatione.
>
> RECVRSAT He has excellently used the frequentative form in the frequent thoughts of the lover.

Again a fairly elementary note (also involving the commendation of the adverb *bene*), once more indicative of the range of audience which Servius keeps in mind.

> 4. GENTIS non Aeneae, ut sit velut excusatio, sed Dardani a numinibus aut Veneris.
>
> 4. GENTIS Not of Aeneas (so that it would be some sort of excuse), but of Dardanus, descended from gods, or of Venus.

Another example of the short, glossing comment of the sort which reappears as a marginal or interlinear note in so many manuscripts of Virgil.

> INFIXI PECTORE VVLTVS VERBAQUE tale et illud est (83) *illum absens absentem auditque videtque.*
>
> INFIXI PECTORE VVLTVS VERBAQVE This is the same sort of thing as [line 83] "when separated from him she still hears him and sees him."

This form of explanation, by cross-reference to another passage in the immediate vicinity of the text, is one of Servius's favorite, and often most effective, methods of explication.

> 5. NEC PLACIDAM MEMBRIS DAT CVRA QVIETEM aut penitus quiete caruit, ut 'placida' epitheton sit quietis, aut habuit quidem quietem, sed non placidam, id est, turbatam somniis; unde et ipsa paulo post (9) *quae me suspensam insomnia terrent.*
>
> 5. NEC PLACIDAM MEMBRIS DAT CVRA QVIETEM Either she went entirely without sleep, so that *placida* is an epithet of sleep; or, while she did enjoy sleep, it was not calm. That is, it was disturbed by dreams. Hence she herself says a little later "what dreams disturb and terrify me."

An interesting remark, which raises the question whether Virgil is using an adjective in a purely descriptive sense, or putting a much more discriminating emphasis upon it. Once more, it is noticeable that Servius presents it as an open question ("either A or B"), which leaves it to the readers to come to their own conclusions. As has already been seen, this is a marked counterbalance to the authoritarian manner he so often assumes.

> 6. POSTERA PHOEBEA LVSTRABAT LAMPADE TERRAS circumlocutio orientis diei — secundum enim et tertium librum Aeneas per noctem in convivio Didonis narraverat — licet, ut supra diximus, Vergilius ista quae per naturam necesse est fieri plerumque contemnat.
>
> 6. POSTERA PHOEBEA LVSTRABAT LAMPADE TERRAS A periphrastic description of the day's rising; for Aeneas had given his narrative of books two and three through

the night — although, as we have said above, Virgil often does not concern himself with what must happen in the natural order of things.

Once again, the magisterial "as we have said above" [i.e., on *Aen.* 1.223] is used to impress upon the reader the abiding importance of this theme throughout our reading of Virgil. This observation on the poet's description of dawn clearly invites the reader to consider the many other ways in which this event is described, and to admire the astonishing variety found in Virgil's expressions.

LVSTRABAT aut 'inlustrabat', aut re vera 'lustrabat', id est 'purgabat'; nam nox quodamodo polluit mundum.

LVSTRABAT Either "shed light upon," or truly *lustrabat*, that is "purified." For in a sort of way night pollutes the world.

This is the third example in six lines of Servius's offering the reader a choice of explanations. As so often, his apparent uncertainty has the effect of enriching our reading of Virgil.

7. **VMENTEM VMBRAM** quia nox omnis umida est, ut (G. I 290) *noctis lentus non deficit umor.* et nihil interest utrum umbram an noctem dicat; nox enim umbra terrae est, ut supra (II 251) *involvens umbra magna terramque polumque.* est etiam hysteroproteron in sensu; Aurora enim solem praecedit.

7. **VMENTEM VMBRAM** Because all night is moist, as [*Georgics* 1.290] "the gentle moisture does not fail the nights." And it makes no difference whether he says "shade" or "night;" for night is the shade of the earth,

as above [*Aen.* 2.251] "wrapping the earth and sky in deep shade." There is also a hysteroproteron in the meaning; for dawn comes before the sun.

This is one of the vast number of Servian notes which reappear in Isidore of Seville's *Etymologiae* [5.31.3]. As so often, while keeping close to his source, Isidore introduces a slight variation to impress his own stamp upon the words. Here Servius's *nox umbra terrae est* becomes Isidore's *umbra terrae noctem facit*, and, when he also repeats the cross-reference to *Aen.* 2.251, Isidore displays his erudition by including part of the previous line as well.

Servius rightly makes much use of figures of speech and thought (here "hysteroproteron"), and clearly expects his readers to have such Greek technical terms at their fingertips.

8. CVM SIC VNANIMEM de re pudenda locuturam parum fuerat sororem eligere nisi etiam unanimem. dicimus autem et 'unanimus' et 'unanimis', sicut 'inermus' et 'inermis'.

8. CVM SIC VNANIMEM When she was intending to talk about an embarrassing matter, it would not have been enough to choose her sister, if she had not also been a "soulmate." We say both *unanimus* and *unanimis*, just as *inermus* and *inermis*.

This interest in variant adjectival forms is pervasive in Servius, with comment on these particular words occurring also in his notes on *Aen.* 1.484; 10.571; 10.750; and reappearing in Isidore's *Etymologiae* 10.90.

MALE SANA non plene sana, amore vitiata; 'male' enim

plerumque 'non', plerumque 'minus' significat, sicut 've', ut 'vecors', 'vesanus'. quamquam 'male' et 'perniciose' significat, ut Lucanus *sic male deseruit.*

MALE SANA Not completely sane, corrupted by love. For *male* often means "not," often "less," just as *ve* in *vecors, vesanus.* Although it can sometimes means "badly" and "destructively," as Lucan [9.310] *sic male deseruit.*

This concern with the negating force of *male* has already appeared in Servius's comment on *Aen.* 2.23, where he has also used the same quotation from Lucan's *Pharsalia* to illustrate his remarks. There seems to be no consistency in the way he will sometimes deliberately refer the reader back to a previous note ("as we have said above"), at other times present his remarks as if he had never made them before.

9. INSOMNIA TERRENT et 'terret' et 'terrent' legitur. sed si 'terret' legerimus, *insomnia* erit vigilia; hoc enim maiores inter vigilias et ea quae videmus in somnis interesse voluerunt, ut 'insomnia' generis feminini numeri singularis vigiliam significaret, 'insomnia' vero generis neutri numeri pluralis ea quae per somnum videmus, ut (VI 896) *sed falsa ad caelum mittunt insomnia manes.* sciendum igitur quia, si 'terret' dixerimus, antiqua erit elocutio; 'insomnia' enim, licet et Pacuvius et Ennius frequenter dixerit, Plinius tamen exclusit et de usu removit. sed ambiguitatem lectionis haec res fecit, quod non ex aperto vigilasse se dixit, sed habuisse quietem inplacidam, id est somniis interruptam, ut intellegamus eam et insomniis territam et propter terrorem somniorum vigilias quoque perpessam.

> 9. INSOMNIA TERRENT The readings *terret* and *terrent* are both found. But if we read *terret*, *insomnia* will mean "sleeplessness." For earlier writers made the following distinction between *insomnia* = "sleeplessness" and *insomnia* = "the things we see in sleep:" *insomnia* as a feminine singular noun means "sleeplessness," but *insomnia* as a neuter, plural noun means "the things we see in sleep." So [*Aen.* 6.897] *sed falsa ad caelum mittunt insomnia manes*. One should realize, therefore, that if we say *terret*, it will be an older form of expression. For although both Pacuvius and Ennius frequently used the word *insomnia* [i.e., the feminine singular noun], yet Pliny excluded it and banished it from use. But the uncertainty about the reading is occasioned by the fact that she does not say openly that she was sleepless, but that she had a disturbed sleep, that is, a sleep interrupted by dreams. So we understand both that she was terrified by dreams, and that because of being terrified by her dreams she also suffered sleeplessness.

This is one of the many fascinating passages in which Servius alludes to textual variants which were already current in his time. Our manuscripts, in fact, unanimously read *terrent* (which is clearly correct), and Servius is the only source for the singular variant *terret*.

This doubt leads him to investigate the reasons behind it, hence the comparatively lengthy weighing of *insomnia/insomnium*. He is, as so often, alert to the changing fashions in language, and illustrates the use of *insomnia* as a feminine singular noun by reference to the two early Latin writers Pacuvius and Ennius (unfortunately without any citation).

The opposing view, that of Pliny the Elder (a frequent authority in Servius), is presented without comment. The lack of specific reference to Pacuvius and Ennius raises the question which comes to mind so frequently throughout the *Commentaries*: is Servius simply lifting this piece of information from an earlier work, or did he find such usages by his own reading of the actual works of these and similar authors?

> 10. NOVVS magnus, ut (E. III 86) *Pollio et ipse facit nova carmina.*

> 10. NOVVS "Great," as [*Eclogues* 3.86] *Pollio et ipse facit nova carmina.*

Another simple glossing note, which actually occurs in a dozen other places in Servius.

> SVCCESSIT SEDIBVS ut (II 723) *succedoque oneri* et (II 478) *succedunt tecto et flammas ad culmina iactant.*

> SVCCESSIT SEDIBVS As [*Aen.* 2.723] *succedoque oneri* and [*Aen.* 2.478] *succedunt tecto.*

A plain and simple grammatical note. The point at issue can be seen by the comment on *Aen.* 2.478, where we are told that the normal construction is *succedo sub* with the accusative case, and that the use of the simple dative case, without any preposition, is "a figure." As this usage of *succedo* with the dative case is frequent from the first century B.C. on, Servius's need to comment presumably reflects a shift in the Latin of his own day.

Conclusion

LOOKING BACK OVER EVEN SO SHORT A SELECTION from the vast *Commentaries*, one is struck by the great breadth of Servius's interests. They range from the purely grammatical or linguistic (notes which are always felt to be necessary to aid the reader's understanding of the very words used by Virgil) to much broader questions of style and imagery. Philosophy, religion, and above all mythology are not represented in the above selection.

The tone of these comments is perpetually interesting, moving, as they do, from the implacably magisterial ("Some people foolishly believe...") to the remarkably flexible ("This can mean either A or B or C"). Yet we should never lose sight of the fact that Servius is always in control, always talking to an audience which is clearly his inferior in learning and therefore in authority.

But above all, there is the abiding passion felt for what he is doing, and the unwavering belief that what he is doing is of the highest importance. These twin strands of authority and passion surely contributed not a little to the overwhelming dominance of Servius in Virgilian studies for so many centuries. Even today one ignores him at one's own risk.

Servius and Commentary on Virgil is the fifth in a series of occasional publications arising from lectures at the Center for Medieval and Renaissance Studies (CEMERS) at the State University of New York at Binghamton. This volume is is the first published by Pegasus Press at the University of North Carolina at Asheville. The series was designed to make available to broad audience studies on a wide variety of subjects by leading medieval and Renaissance scholars.

The study provides a lively introduction to a figure of immense importance for medieval and Renaissance culture and for classical studies. Marshall illustrates several important aspects of Servius's commentary and its *fortuna*, pointing out just where Servius's authority lay — in his teaching of the teachers for centuries. He demonstrates the surprising breadth and variety of Servius's interests as commentator, the passion which informs his wrirting, and the authority which his commentary won and maintained for centuries. One appendix provides a brief view of what we know about Servius himself; another appendix shows Servius at work, presenting and discussing samples of his commentary on the first ten lines of the fourth book of the *Aeneid* and discussing these.

Peter K. Marshall is a distinguished classicist and scholar of the classical tradition in the Middle Ages and Renaissance. Professor of Greek and Latin at Amherst College and a leading authority on Servius, Marshall has published numerous articles and editions — e.g., Aulus Gellius (Oxford Classical Texts), and Cornelius Nepos and Servatus Lupus (Teubner). He is also senior editor of both the *Harvard Servius* and the Servius volume in the *Catalogus translationum et commentariorum*.

ISBN 1-889818-03-8

The Aldo S. Bernardo Fund

The Aldo S. Bernardo Fund is the endowment fund for the Center for Medieval and Renaissance Studies at the State Univer-sisty of New York at Binghamton. Established in 1989 by a gift from the founding co-director of the Center, the Fund aims to support Center programs with a special emphasis on Medieval and Renaissance Italian studies. The governing body of the fund, working with the Executive Council of the Center, has determined that the Bernardo Fund will first support a lecture program and book purchases for the Bartle Library. As the endowment develops, it will support the broad range of programs associated with the Center's teaching and research activities.

The foundation of the State University of New York at Binghamton, which is a private, not-for-profit corporation chartered under the laws of the State of New York receives tax-deductible donations on behalf of the Bernardo Fund.